MW00582300

BÔ YIN RÂ

THE MEANING
OF THIS LIFE

For more information about the books
of Bô Yin Râ and titles published
in English translation, visit
The Kober Press web site at
www.kober.com.

BÔ YIN RÂ
(J. A. SCHNEIDERFRANKEN)

THE MEANING
OF THIS LIFE

TRANSLATED BY
B.A. REICHENBACH

THE
KOBER
PRESS

BERKELEY, CALIFORNIA

For permission to quote or excerpt, write to:

THE KOBER PRESS
2534 Chilton Way
Berkeley, California 94704

or email: koberpress@mindspring.com

This book is a translation from the German of *Der Sinn des Daseins* by Bô Yin Râ, first published in 1927. The copyright to the German original is held by Kober Verlag AG, Bern, Switzerland.

Printed in the United States of America

Library of Congress Catalog Number: 98-067456

International Standard Book Number: 0-915034-06-9

Book cover after a design by Bô Yin Râ

Typesetting and design by Irene Imfeld, Berkeley, CA

CONTENTS

CHAPTER ONE

A CALL
TO THE LOST

Y OU HAVE GROWN tired from your endless searches and now are weary even of that search itself.

Since what you sought was nowhere to be found, you henceforth are no longer willing to pursue your quest.

You once had hoped to find the Spirit's world, the kingdom of the living, and its Temple of Eternity.

But no matter where you turned and searched, you found all realms were subject to the reign of—death. And every temple, in its inmost shrine, enclosed no more than yet another hollow idol.

It is no wonder you lost heart on such a quest. Even as so many others had grown weary, like yourself, who once had set out on their own pursuit with every confidence and full of hope.

Still, one ought not to reproach you, nor must your soul be frightened by accusing words; for it was not your fault if on your journeys through so many distant lands you never found what you had long so ardently desired.

One had instructed you to follow paths that those who sent you forth had not been able to pursue themselves.

You had been promised great rewards, which those who made such promises had never gained themselves.

One had allowed you to continue in a quest whose purpose those directing you had long ago abandoned in defeat.

How, then, could you have known fulfillment where others had experienced only disappointment after disappointment, until at last exhaustion forced them to turn back?

Assuming, they had even tried to go the way they had encouraged you to follow.

How, indeed, could you have ever reached the goal you had desired to attain—by following such hopeless paths?

YET HARBOR NO resentment toward those who gave you false directions; for they themselves had nothing else to give you, seeing that they did not know the way that truly leads you to your goal.

When they told you, "What you seek is found in that direction!" or, "The goal you would attain lies there!" most of them believed that their advice was good.

Even if they counseled you to follow paths which they themselves were forced to give up in despair, they yet believed that you might well succeed where their own strength had failed.

If, on the other hand, you were the victim of a self-deluded dreamer craving power, or of a scoundrel who knew very well that he was leading you astray, then thank your lucky stars that you have finally regained your freedom from such bondage. But even here you should not sit in judgment of another, because the person whom you would condemn has long been judged already—by the verdict of his deeds.

Nor should you quarrel with your fate, given that it did not let you find till now what you had sought. And, least of all, revile yourself if, weary and dispirited, you stand again exactly at the very place where you had once begun your quest so full of hope and confidence.

What profit is there now in accusations and lament?

Besides, the day these words have come into your hands you have no longer any cause to scorn your fruitless searching in the past.

Rest assured that, from this day, the way you follow shall be blest; nor shall you ever be misled again, pursuing paths that end in error.

Today you hear the voice of someone who has knowledge of the way that leads you to your goal.

The voice of one who is not only capable of showing you that way, but who will gladly guide you, so that you may at last attain the goal you had so long pursued in vain.

Follow me, and you shall feel your strength increasing with each step. And thus you will grow strong enough to stay your course until you reach your goal.

It was not *I* who went in search of *you*. Nor is it me you ought to thank for having found my guidance at this time.

Your own determined searching, which had so long pursued mistaken paths, at last was freed from bondage—once you had released it, having tired of its weight.

Now that your will to search is free again, it lets you find what you had failed to see before.

It was entirely your own resolve, your earnest will to search, which of necessity has brought you to discover me.

It was not all in vain, however, that until now your searching was directed toward mistaken paths.

7

Nor was it all for nothing that you followed teachings which could never lead you to your goal.

Wherever you pursued your searches, your very quest lent strength to your pursuit; much as a copper coil intensifies electric current through resistance. And now that you were close to cursing all your past endeavors as pure waste, you finally attained what you had no more even dared to hope.

In the domain of Spirit, where all of us who live on earth are rooted in the selfsame life —be it consciously or not—your soul's distress has been observed. And in that realm one also knew how you might best be given help.

To that end, however, I was sent your way— and you, indeed, have found me—for I can truly help you in your need. Nor is there any other in your present form of life through whom you might receive such help as I can bring you.

This state of things is, surely, not my doing. On the other hand, I cannot change what I myself did not bring into being. However, you would try in vain to interfere with laws that are established; and vain would be your efforts to find other help.

You have been calling me, yet without knowing who I am.

My words today have reached you, without my knowing who you are.

Again, you cannot know as yet who in effect is speaking to you through these words. And thus I surely would not blame you for being still suspicious and hesitant to trust my voice, given that you suffered many disappointments and are embittered by the anguish you experienced in the past.

You are much like a traveler, lost at night within a forest, who hears the calling of a guide who knows the way, but whom at first he fears and seeks to flee because it is a place where many have been robbed and killed.

Were I in your position, I too would surely have profound misgivings!

Consider, though, that all I ask of you is that you carefully watch every step, while following the light that I shall hold before you.

I raise that light ahead of you, so that you clearly can discern with your own eyes wherever I shall lead you.

How I myself gained knowledge of the way, and why it is that at this age there is no other who can show it, are questions that need not concern you at this time.

Content yourself for now with your becoming soon aware of how my guidance clears a path that leads you out of darkness and confusion.

Countless times you may have been betrayed before: this time, however, you shall not become a victim of deceit.

Already as you take your first few steps you will become aware that falsehood and deceit are things you never could encounter on the way that I shall show you.

Until today you could feel justified to scoff at anyone who told you there could be a person who knew about the way that leads to final truth; a guide who was prepared to offer you his help.

Today, you have encountered precisely such a guide.

Now it is yourself who must decide whether you are ready to accept my guidance.

The choice is yours alone; for no one else can answer the question whether you still deem it worth your effort truly to attain—at last—the highest goal you once had sought, but which until this day you always had pursued in vain.

CHAPTER TWO

THE INIQUITY
OF THE FATHERS

Truly, you appear a riddle to yourself; a riddle you have not yet learned to solve.

To be sure, from childhood on you had your teachers, and thus you learned how others at one time had solved the riddle which they, too, had faced within themselves. Yet even so, there came a day for you when all the answers found by others only raised new questions in your mind.

You had wanted to find peace within yourself, yet in your search became increasingly aware that all the answers which in bygone days had satisfied the human mind could not be of much help to you today.

Weary and disheartened you thus gave up the search for answers to the riddle of your life.

You now have come to the conclusion, which you regard as certain "knowledge," that in this present life you never can receive the answer you had sought: an answer that would lead you to abiding peace.

And yet, my friend, you shall indeed find such an answer.

I will gladly show you how you yourself are able to unravel the mystery that is your life.

But to that end you first must come to recognize that proper answers can only be expected from asking proper questions. And so it follows that the many whom you hear complaining because they never found the answers they had sought, rather should deplore the fact that they had never found the proper way to ask their questions.

Today you are embittered, because you, too, have still not found the answers you had so long desired. But never did it cross your mind to wonder whether you, in fact, had asked the proper questions.

Time after time you had to face the bitter truth that all the answers found by others had failed to bring you inner peace. Nonetheless, the wrong approach those others used in asking questions you readily adopted as your own—without concern or second thought.

How could you hope to find your own conclusive answers by following the false example set by others?

How did your mind become entangled in the notion that asking questions in the manner of those others might nonetheless, in your case, lead to real answers? Answers different from those they had themselves received, but which had failed to bring you inner peace?

You see, my friend, the suffering that you endure today descends from the "iniquity" committed by your "fathers." And only you can now atone for their transgression; for you alone are able to become your fathers' savior and redeemer.

What your forebears once had deemed sufficient to secure their own contentment has now become the very cause that undermines your inner peace.

Your forebears, too, had once experienced their existence as a riddle; a mystery for which they found their own solution. However, their solution is now for you a burden and a yoke.

Answers they had once accepted for themselves they left you as their legacy. Only it became a legacy that was to stir new questions in your mind.

But at the same time you inherited a method of inquiry that never shall produce the kind of answer through which your every doubt would dissipate like morning mist before the rising sun.

If you would not remain a riddle to yourself forever, you will have to renounce a legacy that now can only prove your spiritual undoing.

From now on you will have to ask your questions in a new and different way. Nor must the answers that convinced your forebears cause you to inquire in the manner they had done.

You cannot ever find the inner peace for which you long until you shall have learned to ask your questions in a way that is entirely your own.

FROM NOW ON, then, do not inquire any longer about the "God" your forebears used to worship, but seek, instead, the *Living God* abiding in your own eternal soul.

Ask no longer whether life as such has any "worth," but rather seek what worth you can yourself bestow upon your life.

Ask no longer whether there is any "meaning" to existence, but rather how your own existence might gain meaning through yourself.

Ask no longer, "What is Man?" but whether, as a human individual, you truly are yourself what you are capable of being.

Ask no longer, "Is there an immortal soul?" but search, instead, for that in you which manifests your timeless soul, and how you might grow conscious of its presence.

Ask no longer, "Does human life continue after death?" but rather seek what you can do in this your present life in order to attain self-knowing consciousness in your eternal form.

Ask no longer, "What is truth?" but whether you yourself are true in mind and soul and willing not to suffer anything within yourself which might becloud that inner truth.

If you will frame your questions in this way, whatever you may ask is certain to receive an answer. And with that answer you indeed shall find the inner peace that you so ardently desire.

MANY THINGS HAVE mortal minds already sought to know which are in fact quite needless.

Thinkers, thus, were led to fashion answers they believed conclusive, although they merely served appearance. But each of these apparent answers was bound to raise new questions, even if they surfaced to bewilder only later generations.

If you continue asking questions in this way, you shall not only find yourself beset by ever new enigmas, but also leave a wealth of open questions to posterity; especially where you believed your way of finding answers was productive.

Take care, therefore, that every question weighing on your mind will always find in you the proper form in which it need be asked; the form that of necessity presents you with the answer that shall truly satisfy your need—an answer that is yours alone.

For no one else can ever offer you the answer you alone must find.

Only in the form of individual experience can you attain your own conclusive answer; and the experience of that answer you can encounter only in yourself.

ALL THE EXPLANATIONS that common usage treats as "answers" in respect to "final things" —including even words of an authority whom later generations came to worship as a "God" —continue to give rise to further questions, which every age is doomed to ask anew.

Such "answers" can at best encourage you to find within yourself a way of questioning that leads you to the kind of answer one possesses as *experience*.

The fathers of your faith, by contrast, were convinced—and many since have shared that firm conviction—that the verbal definitions which had satisfied their searching minds, were henceforth to be recognized as final and unquestionable "truth." And so they deemed it blasphemy or folly if anyone still dared to ask for other answers.

They may, perhaps, have acted in good faith, convinced they were bequeathing to posterity a heritage of truth and blessing.

But you, my friend, have now learned amply, through your own experience, how fatefully this heritage is haunted by a curse.

Today, it rests with you to break the power of that curse.

However, you can do this only if you will not simply, without scrutiny, transmit to others the solutions which your forebears once had fashioned to explain their life's enigma to themselves. Nor ought you to expect that those who trust your every word should treat the answers you attained as if they also were their own.

Once you find the answer in yourself that grants you inner peace, you ought to use your knowledge only to help others find their own approach to asking questions in themselves.

Be sure that you will always ask your questions in such a way that you must, of necessity, receive the proper answer, which then will truly be beyond all doubt—for you. Do not assume, however, that others now need merely to adopt the answer you received in order to possess your answer as their own.

Every soul that lives on earth with you today, and all who shall live after you in ages yet to come, will have to learn the art of asking their own questions. And in their own unique experience shall all then comprehend the answer to the final questions behind their individual existence.

But those who found the answer to the riddle they had once confronted in themselves should try to caution others not to think that any human mortal could ever solve the mystery of someone else's life.

They should only warn, however, where they perceive the danger that seeking souls are led astray by trusting in the heritage and errors of the fathers.

CHAPTER THREE

THE
HIGHEST GOOD

H ERE, THEN, it is fitting that we speak about the highest good that you possess. For only that which you alone indeed possess, a good belonging to no other, and one no power on this earth could ever wrest from you is, in the end, *your highest good.*

You are yourself that highest good—within that inmost sanctum of your soul that no one else can ever enter. A good that even you can fathom only through *experience*, because your thoughts shall never comprehend it.

You feel your own existence as a conscious "self." Only you may still not be aware that everything which until now you feel as being your true "self" is but the pallid glimmer of a radiant light, emitted by your timeless essence, but then obscured behind the darkening clouds which even your most lucid thinking leaves behind.

At rare and hallowed moments only will this radiance of your real nature pervade all darkness in your being and find its way into your mental consciousness, which then feels frightened by that presence, as by a wholly foreign life.

And yet, this radiant essence, which you on such occasions suddenly perceive—and then interpret to yourself as some sublime external force—is, in reality, your own, most personal possession.

Whatever else within your nature you look upon as being "yours" can be reclaimed from you at any moment; for you possess it only briefly, the while you live your fleeting days on earth.

Nothing but this absolute reality—from all eternity begotten in the Spirit by the Spirit—will come to be your own forever, once your awakened consciousness has knowingly received it in itself.

From this alone you may conclude that nothing but this one sublime reality is rightly to be judged your highest good. Even though your mortal mind may well conceive of other things it would deem worthy of that rank.

YET AT THIS POINT you still are unaware of how you might make use of that sublimest good, which you possess within yourself.

You are, to use an image, like the heir to an enormous fortune whom eccentric cruelty has caused to be brought up in abject poverty, to keep him ignorant of his potential wealth. And now he innocently begs his bread where he in truth is lord and master of the land.

Indeed, your life on earth remains forever meaningless, if you will not *yourself* inform it with this meaning: that it will let you recognize your everlasting highest good, by virtue of its contrast with the countless phantom goods you only *seem* to own in this dimension of appearance.

You must, of course, be willing to perceive and learn what your existence here on earth is able to reveal to your experience.

You must not let your phantom goods possess you so completely that they are bound
to suffocate all higher longings of your soul;
longings which could still awaken the spiritual energies you need if you would finally
dispel the mental clouds created by your
earthbound murky thinking, in order to lay
hold of that within yourself which you shall
own forever, the moment you have claimed
it, having proved yourself its rightful heir.

Until today you have allowed the "focal
point," the center of your consciousness, to
be displaced, somewhere outside your real
self.

Take care, my friend, to move that "focus"
back again, to where it was in the beginning,
eternities ago, and where it then shall
rest forever: within the self that you alone
possess.

For, come the day when you must leave this
present life—no matter how tenaciously you
cling to its imagined phantom goods—the
"focus" of your being would otherwise be
out of reach, lost in the eternal Void. And
only after aeons suffered in despair would

you be able to perceive it once again within your own eternal self.

It is much easier than you might think to find your way back to your inmost self while you still live your life on earth, and thus to grow aware of your essential being in the realm where you are truly in your timeless home.

To be sure, this self-discovery is clearly not the union with your *Living God,* which you are one day to attain. However, you cannot experience your own self in God, united with God's essence, unless you first shall have awakened, as a conscious spiritual being, within your own eternal life.

Toward that eternal, inmost nature must all your self-awareness turn its will, if you would see your present life acquire meaning—through yourself.

You shall attain the goal you seek if you are able—notwithstanding all the happiness that you enjoy in mortal life—to keep at all times conscious of the fact that there abides in you still something other: a life that far surpasses anything you ever could encounter in your outer world, and that this hidden "other" is in truth your own eternal self.

Your real "self" is truly something "other" in respect to your external world, but also in regard to that which you, as part of this external world, assume to be your "real" self.

When, in your present state of self-awareness, you say "I," the content of that self-expression is determined purely by components that must one day disintegrate and perish. Having once regained your inmost self, within the focal center of your conscious life, you will be able to say "I" exactly as before, but now the content of that self-awareness, which you will then find very strange and new, shall be composed of only elements imperishable and eternal, scarcely even touched by things that, in your mortal outer life, continue to be subject to decay and death.

Nor is it different for one whose consciousness already has been unified with God when he says "I." Only in his case the content of that "I" is at the same time inwardly illuminated by the Godhead's light, through which the human soul's eternal core is set ablaze, as is a diamond by the sun.

BE NOT DELUDED by accounts of people who believed that they were "one with God" in moments of ecstatic rapture, because they failed to apprehend their own eternal nature, owing to their false approach, and thus mistook their inmost self for something outside their own being.

Spellbound in their ecstasy, they saw their own selves as some other being. And this unsettling vision appeared to them so awesome and sublime that they could not conceive of any explanation other than to think that God himself must have descended and appeared within their soul.

Delusions of that kind have flourished throughout history and can be found among all nations of the earth.

Sprouting more abundantly than meadow saffrons on a marshy pasture do people who exhibit such alleged "gifts" emerge among believers of a certain orientation even now, yet few are those who chance to find their own biographer to chronicle their visions.

You, HOWEVER, should instead be guided by the tried and tested knowledge that all *authentic* spiritual perception, which apprehends the realm of *absolute reality,* is only witnessed in the form of fully independent "self"-experience.

Be warned of every "other," whom you cannot see, but who attempts to capture your attention, be it in the guise of acting as your "guide," or even speaking as the "voice of God."

You may, without exception, in all such cases rest assured that in this way you never shall receive *authentic* guidance from the Spirit's world.

I would not have you stand in fear before all things invisible, but here it is my duty to warn you clearly of grave danger. And if you would know more about the things that here I only touch upon, you will find other places in my writings where these matters are discussed in more detail.

Let it suffice you here if I assure you that everything proceeding from God's Spirit shall enter your perception only through your inmost being, and that you likewise will perceive and apprehend the Spirit's message only through your timeless self, in your eternal nature.

At such a time you then shall clearly feel "I know!" But now that sense of knowing will differ quite profoundly from the way you used to "know," when all your knowledge issued merely from your own endeavors and resources.

There now is something that will "speak" in you, but you will hear that "speaking" only in the innermost of your eternal nature, the realm where your abiding spiritual self will share with you the insights it is granted in the Spirit's world.

It is likewise only in this way that one is able, from the Spirit's world, to lend you the discernment that you need in order to distinguish clearly between *objective* spiritual realities and the *subjective* phantoms of your own excitable imagination.

Nor is it different for any person who is able to perceive the Spirit's world objectively, when its realities transform themselves before him to the point of visible concreteness.

In the perception of the Spirit's life, the will of such a person remains at all times *active*.

Insights that in truth originate within the Spirit's world will never force themselves upon the consciousness of the observer.

Although a person still may lack the power to select the things he wishes to perceive, everyone who can in fact behold the Spirit's world is nonetheless aware that he remains at all times free not only to receive the Spirit's revelations, but also to effect their instant disappearance, in case they are not needed.

A visual experience originating in the Spirit's realm, whose substance is self-conscious light, could never "haunt" a human soul. Nor would it ever manifest itself unwanted, against a person's will, when his attention is absorbed by other things.

Whoever senses some coercion connected with his inner seeing may be quite certain that the things he sees do not originate in the dimension of the Spirit's life, even if it would appear that they could only stem from the sublimest realms of inner light.

Concerning this, the world today is still deluded by a fateful misconception, whose effects continue even now to bury almost every testimony of objective truth from ancient times with heavy coats of clinging mud.

One day it shall be recognized again that people in the ancient world were not naively superstitious when they judged it possible that human beings could become "possessed." Once that fact is understood, however, not a few of the ideas and doctrines that nowadays still lurk in human minds will find themselves unmasked as plain examples of such physical possession.

IF YOU, a reader seeking light, intend to find the highest good within yourself, you must at all times bear in mind that you can only reach that goal in total freedom of your self-determination.

You are at liberty to seek that goal, and you are able, in the end, to find it. However, you are no less free to pass it by without a thought.

Yet if you are resolved to seek your highest good within, be sure to keep yourself at all times free of any kind of domination by those dark, though hidden powers that ever lie in wait in the unseen dimension of this world, eager to enslave a human being's will and to consume his soul.

These predators form part of the invisible dimension which surrounds the world of matter, and all the miracles and wondrous feats which they are able to perform are nothing more than *physical* events, confined entirely within the hidden side of nature.

But they will shrink from nothing wherever they are able to impose their will upon a human soul, and frequently will even drain their victim's physical capacities and strength.

Keep your distance when at times you see that people here and there devoutly worship things they cannot understand—treating them as holy because they seem incomprehensible—and if they then infer, from such external observation, that here the "Spirit of eternal truth" had visibly revealed its power: by working magic sleight of hand.

In yourself alone shall you one day experience the one authentic miracle; provided you are able to advance yourself sufficiently to cause that miracle to happen.

Only in yourself—within the inmost center of your being—you finally possess your highest good. And it embraces everything that grants you inner peace.

The power to decide your life is now placed in your hands. Thus, you may indulge your present self by letting it experience this external world, and merely stay a phantom image in a world of phantoms. Or, you may determine to become, and to remain for all eternity, your true and real self, awakened in your highest good.

Even now—within your present physical existence—you can discover your *eternal life*. And all authentic sages of the past have always promised you precisely that; for they themselves had found that life within them. And, truly, only then shall you be able to experience the joys and happiness your earthly life can offer you—without misgivings and remorse.

CHAPTER FOUR

THE "EVIL" INDIVIDUAL

FROM ANCIENT TIMES we have the words of one who had no better things to say about his fellow mortals than that "the heart of man is evil from his youth."

But you would truly have to be a thoroughly embittered parent if you were to agree with such a bleak assessment.

If you yourself are not by nature "evil," you doubtless will discover "good" things also in your child. And so you need not first implant by *education* what your child possesses as a gift from birth.

Indeed, you well may come to recognize that even the supposed "evil" observed in the behavior of a child is not the work of evil will, but can be easily explained in other ways.

If you would pass fair judgment in these matters you must proceed with caution; nor should you trust your preconceived ideas.

It would, of course, be foolish if one attempted to deny, or casually dismiss, the actual reality of evil, such as it later may reveal its presence in a human being.

And yet, what is this kind of "evil" other than the obvious *degeneration* of a drive inherent in the animal component found in human nature?

You surely would not call the instinct of self-preservation an "evil" drive as such, only because it may turn into evil once it has in fact *degenerated*.

Even in his fellow creatures, whose nature man so scrupulously wants to see distinguished from the animal component in himself, the human mind assumes it has detected "evil." For, in the end, one could not help but recognize some "human" traits in animal behavior, and thus mistakenly imputed human motives and emotions to the natural instincts active in the creature world.

But if you will examine things more closely, you may quite easily convince yourself that here it would be wrong to speak of "evil," because the instinct of survival, even though it manifest itself in cruel forms, is not by any means degenerate within the animals' domain.

In all your fellow animals you will invariably observe that basic instinct bound by clearly given limits, which are determined in each case by the respective nature of the species.

Among all creatures on this earth, man alone at times tears down the barriers which human beings too, as members of the creature world, are bidden to respect. And only in the human being can the instinct of survival consequently sink to monstrous levels of perversion.

You then will see that instinct spread like a malignancy without restraint, feeding on the human mind's imagination, fattened by its faculty of abstract thought.

When you observe one of your fellow creatures as it torments its prey before at last devouring it, you feel too readily inclined to see in such behavior obvious proof of the inherent "evil" disposition of that animal. Yet in reality you witnessed nothing other than expressions of the creature's joy of having captured food; of holding its elusive quarry in its power; and, finally, of sensing the release of the especial tension resulting either from the strain of having lain in ambush, or the exertion of a heated chase.

Perhaps you heard that some ferocious beasts of prey, once they have been fed, become quite harmless, while others will attack all things alive, even when not hungry.

Still, you ought not to assume an animal is "evil," not even one that seems to kill because of its supposed "thirst for blood"; lest you mistakenly attribute—to that animal's delimited capacities—the gift of spiritual empathy, which only you possess: by virtue of your timeless *human soul*.

One rightly has observed that also animals have "souls." Indeed, this kind of "creature soul," or *psyche,* is present in yourself as well. Still, the substance of that "psyche" is merely *physical,* is matter in a "fluid" state. It must not be confused with man's *eternal soul,* which finds its self-expression only in the human creature's organism, and in conjunction with the latter's "psyche." The human spirit's timeless soul—by contrast with its mortal psyche—is a creation of dynamic elements originating in the all-embracing ocean of the soul within the realm of Spirit.

It is those elements of your *eternal* soul that make you capable of sensing what you believe are the emotions of another being; in that such elements alone allow you to perceive the pain that other beings feel, to "sympathize"—to share the pain—whenever you see fellow creatures suffer.

Your fellow animals may doubtless help each other when they observe one of their kind in need, but they could never *feel* the anguish of the other as *their own.*

The animal knows only: Here is a being like myself in danger! And thus it tries, at best, to save its own kind in the image of the other.

One even finds remarkable attachment in the "psyche" of an animal; no less than fright or sadness, when it detects a fellow creature in distress. And here the animal will also treat the human being simply as a fellow creature like itself. But never can it truly feel "compassion,"—sense the other's pain—however much one might be tempted to believe that certain animals exhibit that capacity.

The dog that will get restless, or even may refuse to eat, because it fears it may have lost its owner, is driven by unconscious care for the familiar human being, whose will and presence it enjoyed to feel. Nonetheless, the dog's behavior is not stirred by pity for its master and need not differ in the least, whether the latter had actually died, or rather merely sold him and still enjoyed the best of health.

Nor is the so-called "cruel" creature somehow gaining pleasure from the pain it is inflicting; for seeking pleasure in another being's anguish always presupposes *empathy*—ability to share the other's feelings—even if that being's suffering is not perceived as pain, but as a form of pleasure.

Likewise, the ferocious hunter that, as humans like to think, kills purely for the sake of "sport" is either merely after blood as a desired kind of food, or anxious to eradicate whatever it perceives as a potential threat. Also, it may simply not be able to control its hunting instinct when it scents its favored prey.

And so you never must accuse an animal, not even the most "vicious," of having done an "evil" deed; nor of deriving pleasure from committing "evil" acts; nor, in the human understanding of the word, of being "evil" by design.

AT TIMES, however, also the "evil" human individual is only the custodian of its inherent instinct of survival, or of the impulse to preserve its kind.

What you are then inclined to judge as "evil" in a person's conduct may still be quite within the bounds that nature has imposed upon the instinct of self-preservation, as well as on the impulse to preserve one's kind.

Only where the human mind has willfully destroyed those bounds will such inherent instincts horribly degenerate.

Nature's drives will then become deformed, changed into obsession to destroy, into compulsion which finds pleasure in the anguish it inflicts on others.

And only here do we in fact encounter *evil* face to face!

For only here is evil brought into existence, generated by a *human will*.

But at this point it had already come into existence—even though not manifest as yet in outer life—because it is in *thought* that every kind of evil first must be conceived and born.

It is as human *thought* that evil first is brought into existence; for only thus can evil thoughts give life, in turn, to evil *words* and *deeds*.

UNDERSTAND THAT evil is against the order underlying nature, and that it has been forced upon her realm by human will alone.

Once the instinct of survival must, of necessity, become an overpowering force, and thus *degenerate,* because the energy of human thought has torn down every barrier intended to confine it—even in the *human* being's creature life—then that instinct unavoidably transforms itself into an evil drive, which finally breeds pleasure by inflicting evil and by making other beings suffer pain.

Among all creatures found within the visible domain of nature, none but the human being introduces evil into this material world.

Man alone—among all creatures one can physically perceive—is capable of generating evil; for only he can tear down, through his thinking, the protective walls that, in the animal domain, enclose and curb the basic instinct of survival.

You now must not assume, however, that "evil" in all forms is limited to merely this material world—the realm your senses can perceive—nor that it can be generated only in the sphere of mortal human action.

Assuming this could prove a fatal error!

Here your caution must extend to the *invisible* domain as well; for what in this external world you apprehend, by virtue of your mortal senses, is in reality the smallest part of physical existence. And, surely, it would be unwise if you were wholly to ignore the sphere that constitutes by far the larger part of physical reality.

Now there is much alive in even the invisible dimension of this world that you would likewise see as "evil," in much the same way you ascribe that trait to certain animals. And yet, in either case it only is the instinct of survival, or the impulse to preserve one's kind, that here is seeking active self-expression.

Other things are here at work besides, rather like the rage of captured animals that struggle to regain the freedom they can see before their eyes, but which they cannot reach.

In addition, there abide in this dimension also beings that, just like human mortals, are capable of breaking down—by force of thought—the barriers imposed upon the instinct of survival. For, in the context of the cosmic order, the faculty of thinking is not by any means confined to only mortal human brains; even though the human being, as a mortal creature here on earth, has access to the force of thought exclusively through that particular organ.

Much like mortal humans, these beings, too, beget and bring into existence "evil" in the realm of thought. But given that, in the invisible dimension, the energy of thought is free of the resistance it encounters when transformed in human minds, it here asserts itself with infinitely greater force.

Indeed, the flood of evil which thus continuously inundates the visible dimension of the planet exceeds all bounds and limits. And while that tide remains concealed from human beings' conscious sense perception, unconsciously they are continuously subject to its influence—and, in the majority of cases, without offering even token resistance.

Regard yourself as fortunate that, in this visible domain at least, you are surrounded by protective barriers and have the power, if you truly are resolved, to save yourself from that deluge of evil by seeking refuge on the high ground of your inner life.

Beware lest you yourself should breach the dam and let the venomous pollution flowing from these hidden sources inundate your present life!

Still, many people breach that dam unwittingly, by virtue of their thinking.

Every thought of malice or of hatred—however hateful you might judge a thing to be—delivers you, without your knowing, into the power of the hidden fiends in the invisible domain of nature.

You then have, by your thinking, summoned them, have paved their way into your life and, rest assured, they know how to infuse the power of their thoughts into your unsuspecting mind.

Countless human souls have thus become "possessed" without discerning their condition. And every day continues to claim more and more such hapless victims.

Yet once this fearsome power holds you in its grip, you have no other way to free yourself but by your constant, firm, and absolute rejection of any thought of hatred, even in its weakest form, no matter who or what might be its object. In short, by your unwavering and categorical refusal to harbor henceforth in your mind even the remotest trace of malice.

THERE ARE doctrines that would have you think all evil in the world is nothing other than "illusion"; for everything that is "must" needs be "good," because all things are, after all, from "God." And "God," according to such doctrines, could not conceivably create but what is "good."

Such notions, to be sure, betray a blithely superficial way of thinking, although some people draw from them the inspiration for a rather carefree style of life.

Minds that can so easily be satisfied with what they call their "knowledge" are much like inexperienced mountain climbers who, knowing nothing of the danger, confidently walk across a snowdrift, a peril every expert would avoid and skirt at a respectful distance.

No doubt, a climber might succeed and make it to the summit even walking over snowdrifts—if, that is, he has more luck than brains, and the unstable bridge does not collapse beneath his weight.

There likewise is a grain of truth embedded even in the mentioned doctrines. And those who can detect that grain at least may use it as a hint to bridge the chasm of enigmas that surround this mortal form of life.

The truth contained within those doctrines comes to this: All evil is engendered only in domains of transient, conditional reality— whether it be in this present life of physical perception, or in dimensions mortal senses cannot apprehend—and that such evil ceases to exist for those who have surmounted such contingent worlds.

On the other hand, if you accept those shallow doctrines literally, in the sense they are proposed, you also must regard all other things surrounding you in life on earth as mere "illusion," including even what is good. You scarcely will deny, however, that notwithstanding such ideas, this world of "nonreality" is capable at times of making you quite painfully aware of its *reality*. Because this world is, after all, by no means merely insubstantial "nothing," a pure mirage one cannot feel; nor is its very *being* or *nonbeing* in the least determined by your will.

Thus, you should not let the faulty logic of such pseudo-wisdom lead your mind astray; for that would by unworthy of your gifts.

You LIKEWISE should reject, however, any doctrine telling you that "evil" is a heritage transmitted to you in your mortal body, a legacy whose consequences you cannot escape.

You well may have inherited the inclination to do evil from your forebears, and now possess it in your blood; but never is the force of evil a *natural* component of your being.

However forcefully the evil bent that you perhaps inherited may tempt you to succumb —as long as you do not associate your will with its allure, it has no power to affect you.

Whoever will fall prey to the destructive cravings active in his blood has frivolously played with his own nature and still is far from recognizing his inherent strength.

The ancestors whose blood is coursing through your veins and who, perhaps, had not been able in their day to master its desires, have most decidedly no power whatsoever to control *your* will.

But now it is your will alone that shall determine whether you are able to become the master of your blood, or will debase yourself to serve it as a slave.

Of course, you here must truly be determined to achieve that goal.

Simply wishful thinking will not effect the least in this pursuit.

When speaking of their "will," most people typically deceive themselves; for what they mean by "will" is either the suggestion of their wishes, or even the particular desires of their blood that need to be subdued by strength of will.

Many hardly sense how greatly they delude themselves when they protest they are "too weak" to stand their ground against the urgings of their blood; even while in every wanton hour they easily might catch themselves deriving pleasure from the very instincts they had wanted to subdue, but which they were in fact indulging in this way.

Countless people frivolously nurse their wishes, despite the fact they know full well that the fulfillment of such wishes can only come about by evil means.

But no sooner have desires and destructive wishes managed to engender evil, and thus brought forth distressing consequences, than those very people will accuse their "fate" and grow unseemly expert in the wretched skill of blaming others for their own mistakes.

MANY A PERSON could forge himself a happier and better fate if only he would, from the first, consistently refuse to make the least concession to the impulse driving him toward evil, as soon as he perceives that inclination even faintly in his mind.

When evil—once engendered in the mental realm—is standing on the threshold of becoming *action,* the human being's strength has in effect been broken; for by that time a person's will already has aligned itself with evil's force.

All resistance then is hopeless and becomes an agony of self-inflicted pain.

Thus, you need to smother the first vague intimation of emerging "evil," before it ever can grow strong enough to stir you as a *feeling,* or even to become a *thought!*

Provided you remain alert, you will not find it difficult to shield yourself from danger.

You need to trust *yourself,* and your own power, the strength of which is greater than all possible temptation.

You were invested with that power for a reason; and if you feel it still is insufficient, you always can increase its strength—by means of constant practice.

If you courageously show faith in your own strength, you also may be confident that spiritual help will come to your assistance.

That inner help shall then be granted you in ways that will unfailingly assure your own ability to *help yourself.*

CHAPTER FIVE

SUMMONS FROM THE WORLD OF LIGHT

I TRUST, MY FRIEND, that you have known those moments in your life, when suddenly, without apparent reason, and even in the midst of teeming crowds, you felt pervaded by a strange sensation of profound detachment from the world surrounding you, while at the same time there awoke in you a nameless kind of longing, which often would remain with you for hours.

Attempting to recall that sense of longing now, you might perhaps describe it in this way:

"It was as if my soul were filled with a mysterious longing for a realm that used to be its timeless home, which it could sense immeasurably far away.

"It was a longing to be close again to beings formed of light; beings who could understand and know the deepest feelings of my heart.

"It may have been the longing for a state of unknown, all-pervading happiness, which nonetheless I felt to be mysteriously familiar."

Perhaps you also were amazed at your experience, since you could not detect what might have been its cause.

Your physical surroundings at the time did not give any indications of its source.

Beyond that world, however, you did not care to probe, for fear you might be led into the shady sphere of superstition.

Thus you preferred to think of your experience as having simply been a "curious mood" and soon lost interest in searching for some explanation.

And yet, there were good reasons to explore the cause of so perplexing an experience. Indeed, had you persisted in your search, you well might have discovered that your sensations had been brought about unknowingly by inner contact with a world you cannot see.

For what you had experienced was nothing less than an authentic glimpse of how the Spirit's world reveals its light, even in the midst of your external life. If at such times all things in your familiar surroundings seemed strangely new and distant, it was because for one brief moment your consciousness was touched by that domain of living light which is your soul's eternal home.

That also is the reason why you felt that spiritual longing; for as the two dimensions came in contact, you recognized instinctively that all of this external world of matter was finally no more to you than a remote, if well-known, foreign land.

I would advise you to pay close attention to such moments in the future, and to accept their gifts with gratitude.

Such moments harbor wondrous energies, which may decisively affect your life on earth.

Your inmost world may find itself profoundly changed if you are willing to pay heed to what such moments grant you.

And if you care to pay attention, you soon will note that such events are likely to recur at certain intervals.

You then shall also note, however, that those intervals continue to grow shorter, the more deeply you revere what you are granted when these worlds come into contact with each other.

There are many trying to detect the world of light, but never come to know it.

However, at such moments anyone can apprehend that inner world; and all alike are granted this experience, even if they never sought it.

Only there are some who feel that, as for them, such an experience hardly is sufficiently momentous; because, as they imagine it, the world of light would have to manifest itself in radiant clarity before they might concede that it exists.

In other words, they want the world of Spirit to reveal itself according to their fancy.

Romantically exalted notions thus prevent them from discerning the elusive intuitions of their heart, through which alone the world of light is able to unveil itself to souls that still are strangers to its nature.

Outlandish fantasies are everywhere in fashion and misbegotten theories intoxicate the minds; and thus it hardly is surprising that so very few attain true knowledge of the world of light, although they have its witness constantly before their eyes.

One is unwilling to accept the fact that spiritual reality could be so very simple.

One would encounter magic powers manifesting their might—in this external world —and feel one's soul consumed with awe. Instead, one senses nothing more than an elusive glimpse of a domain of mysteries and wonders far away.

But if you truly would know certainty in matters of the Spirit, you need to pay attention to the subtle messages your inner life receives.

The world of light is just as close to you as are the things of this material world, but it can never manifest its presence unless you will develop your perceptive faculties, that they may apprehend the immaterial energy that gives that world its substance, breath, and life.

What causes both dimensions to converge is nothing other than the apprehension of the resonance created by the Spirit's radiant substance in your soul, even if your mind cannot explain what you have consciously perceived.

To be sure, there are within you also other matters; realities that want you to experience them far more concretely; but you shall never cross the threshold barring you from knowing such realities unless you learn to heed those quiet intuitions of which I spoke above.

They can arise in you wherever you may be, in every mood and state of mind, provided you are willing to perceive them.

You may experience them at times of deepest grief, but equally in radiant joy; both in the midst of bustling crowds, and in remotest solitude.

At the seashore in a tempest; on mountain peaks; in open fields and in a quiet forest—but also in your home, alone behind closed doors.

A work of art may lift your soul to apprehend the world of light, even as the least of nature's wonders can inspire you to touch that realm.

There is no need to search for any special setting, nor does it call for lengthy preparations.

On the other hand, you would do well to keep yourself at all times firmly at a height that truly justifies your hope of apprehending what is holy.

It is your task to master and make use of this material world, which here is given you the while you live on earth. And you should use it joyfully, with all your senses wide awake. Beware, however, lest you entrap yourself in your external world and thus become your own undoing.

No matter what you may encounter in this outer world, you always must remain in full control of your experience.

Do not become ensnared by false ideas of "freedom," the way one catches birds, with bait in front of hidden nets.

Not all things you permit yourself are things you are permitted!

You cannot bring about the inner "contact" with the world of light if you immerse yourself too much in things that needs must perish and decay, and if you only seek your pleasure.

Being purer than the purest substance found on earth, the world of light cannot combine itself with darkness and corruption.

Nor can you apprehend the world of light, at moments when it touches your external life as long as you are dazed by scintillating phantoms and treasure worldly goods beyond their worth; goods that shall be useless once the bonds are severed that today still bind you to the solid matter of this earth.

However closely you are fettered by material bonds, you nonetheless retain the freedom —for all your physical constraints—to choose your actions wisely.

Among the choices to be faced, in varying external situations, you will from now on learn consistently to choose the one that leads you to a higher level, and to reject whatever will prevent you from remaining at that height.

If you but try to be a little watchful when you make your choice, you shall not ever be in doubt as to the course that you must choose.

It may indeed be said that "opposites converge" when, in your consciousness, the Spirit's world of light encounters the domain of matter. And yet, this contact comes about by virtue only of the elements that both dimensions have in common.

If your awakened consciousness would know the world of truest light, when it perceptibly comes near you in this present life, then your spirit's highest will must resolutely strive toward that elusive realm.

Only that in you which is of kindred nature with the world of light can unify its essence with that radiant sphere.

The world of light will manifest its presence even while there still is nothing yet sufficiently enlightened in your nature to let it be united with the Spirit's light. However, you will not be consciously awake in the domain of light, nor unified with its inherent substance, until that world encounters kindred elements within yourself.

It thus is truly needful that you cultivate and nurture the very highest of your inner qualities. You would, indeed, be well advised to keep your consciousness at all times at its height.

You will from now on have to turn your mind away from everything that is in conflict with your highest nature. And certain things to which, regrettably, you long since have become accustomed will henceforth have to cease—if one day you would consciously awaken in the world of light.

Then, however, you will surely see the day when, full of joy, you shall be capable of comprehending what almost passes comprehension.

All the darkness still surrounding you on earth today shall then have vanished from your sight, penetrated by the radiance of eternal light.

Realities you once had fathomed only vaguely have now become concrete experience.

The world of light, which in the past so often had revealed itself to your perception, only to elude your grasp again and again, will then remain accessible to you at any time, continuously open to your now awakened inner sense.

CHAPTER SIX

THE BENEFITS
OF SILENCE

THOSE WHO WOULD experience inner light, and find the peace the world without can never grant, must learn to practice silence if they intend to make true progress on the journey toward their highest goal.

Many long since would indeed have found that light within them, if only they were able to control their tongue.

Most people seem to think, however, that no event ought to occur within their soul which they should not at once divulge to others, at great length.

The faintest impulse of their wanting to pursue some inner goal is paralyzed, before they even start, by noisily announcing it to all the world. Yet if perchance they do perceive a glimpse of inner life, there is no end to their discussing it until the last effect of the experience has been talked to death—and still their tongue can find no rest.

Like a machine that will not stop, the mind continuously searches for new things that might be said, no matter what the subject.

HERE I AM NOT speaking of the rare exceptions when authentic spiritual guidance may require that the pupil tell his mentor what he has experienced.

In such a case, necessity to speak can prove a valuable factor in the person's schooling, while at the same time other obligations are imposed, which truly call for strictest silence.

But even here the pupil needs to learn to keep his insights from all others.

To no one must they be disclosed but to the guide in whose authority he placed his trust; be it that this helper act according to his proper lights, or under the direction of a higher source.

Only with express permission will a pupil be allowed to speak about his inner life with others who are guided toward the same goal as himself.

Thus it has been since the dawn of time; nor will that practice ever change in all the ages yet to come.

I trust this admonition will be understood by those to whom it is addressed.

To TALK ABOUT pursuing any kind of inner, spiritual quest amounts to an egregious waste of energy while one has not yet actually attained the object of one's search.

Such idle talking may prove still more harmful, however, if a person seeking light reveals what he has found already to his fellow seekers, who are perhaps to know the same experience in a completely different way; for all experience in the Spirit's world remains uniquely *individuated,* and none will be commingled with another.

A garrulous enthusiast who in this manner fails to curb an idle tongue may cause immeasurable harm, both to himself and others.

There is no other field in which the grossest kind of quackery is practiced with such irresponsible naiveté as in the ranks of those who search for light and guidance in the Spirit.

Here, even those incapable of standing on their own two feet feel competent to show the way to others. And no matter how dependent they themselves still are on inner help, they yet believe that only others need assistance.

Such heavy-handed helpfulness is not a little kindled by their mind's unconscious vanity. Yet it is only through the unrestrained loquacity of others that this kind of solicitude receives its sweeping license.

I hope that readers will forgive my calling this compulsive urge to chatter a sort of "verbal dysentery"; for here this drastic image appears distinctly justified.

No one, it would seem, can any longer keep the least thing to himself. And so it hardly is surprising that so few succeed in gaining inner energies as a result of their experiences.

Bookstores have run out of storage space, as every reader of the daily press who deems himself sufficiently informed on any subject today feels called upon to write a book about his views.

Similarly, the majority of those who strive for spiritual light seem to believe that, no sooner have they sensed the faintest ray of inner life, they instantly must broadcast to their "fellow seekers" whatever modest insight they perchance might have received.

The motive that inspires, and continually feeds, this passion to divulge one's inner life is the idea that seekers here can "learn" from one another. What they refuse to recognize is that the goal they are to reach implies a *personal experience,* which is not somehow "learned" from someone else, but has to be encountered and acquired by every person *individually.*

The things which, on the other hand, a person truly has to learn—in order to attain that individual experience—have been stated clearly, through the ages, by those who had authority to offer inner guidance. And in their teaching all of them repeated one requirement: the need to practice silence.

Even when such silence was imposed where it might seem like "secret mongering," the true intent behind the charge must, as a rule, be sought in the enlightened recognition of silence as a potent factor in advancing inner growth.

If a person's spiritual insights are to change the very structure of his soul, so that he will perceive, in light and clarity, what earlier had lain in darkness, then that person's soul must very carefully be guarded, lest its calm should be disturbed.

Indeed, one must not even let one's thoughts concern themselves too noisily with the realities one has perceived within.

Only one who gained perfection in the Spirit's world can know how much may be disclosed. And if a real master came to guide a pupil, he will allow him to reveal no more than what is possible without endangering the pupil's own development, which such disclosures are intended to advance.

Iᶠ ʏᴏᴜ, my friend, would not impede your progress toward your highest goal, you too will have to learn the art of keeping silence.

I see but little use in all your inner searching, in all your tireless activity, if you cannot restrain your idle tongue.

Nor must you practice silence only in respect to others.

Even facing your own self you need to learn observing silence.

What this demands you surely are not able to achieve from one day to the next, and more than one temptation is bound to challenge your resolve.

However, what you here pursue is nothing less than your sublimest goal; and no one ever has attained that highest goal who failed to practice silence.

Countless, on the other hand, are those who cannot curb an idle tongue, but wonder why they have accomplished nothing, even though they feel convinced of having thoroughly fulfilled whatever one could possibly expect of them.

Perhaps they did indeed do much that was correct. And yet they failed in one significant respect; for they had never learned to guard their tongue.

You, however, must not make the same mistake.

Treat it as a sacred duty to perfect yourself in keeping silence.

You hardly can imagine the effectiveness of silence before you learned, from personal experience, that all the energies that form your soul reveal their highest powers only in a state of calm.

Again, your inner life is not the only thing concerning which you should keep silent. Instead, your silence should extend to all things that do not impose the need to speak.

Do not commit the error of so many who rack their brains in search of things they may have left unsaid, but which could still be added. Search, instead, for anything that might gain strength by being left unsaid.

Just how effectively your being silent will increase your inner strength you soon shall learn if you are able, even for an hour, to restrain a word that constantly would cross your lips.

Yet being able to keep silence must not mislead you to indulge in surly muteness, at times when others have the right to hear what you may have to say.

Your silence will prove beneficial to you only if no person ever is aware that you compel yourself to hold your tongue.

Those with whom you are in conversation must not at any time suspect that you are silent on a topic that might well arise, nor must they get a sense of what especial subject you avoid; for otherwise your silence will be meaningless.

Avoid as well the ill-bred kind of muteness that some display without restraint when, in the midst of conversation, their mind becomes absorbed by some idea that needs much time for thought.

The moment when another person may expect to hold your full attention hardly is the proper time to be immersed in probing thoughts.

Your aim to practice silence, then, must never be discernible in your external life, and you alone should be the witness of the secrets you withhold.

You always have to know, of course, when being silent is your right, and when, by contrast, others are entitled to hear you openly express your views.

If you are silent where you ought to speak, you will be guilty of a moral wrong. In addition, the guilt born of that wrong shall weigh on you the heavier, the more you had been conscious of your duty to speak out.

You will be held accountable for both your silence and your speech. Nor is there any sovereignty in heaven or on earth that ever could deliver you from the responsibility you bear for what you do.

Now while your silence, as a factor of your spiritual development, cannot be ranked too highly, you never must forget that here all benefits are turned into their opposite the instant when one person's gain is to be reaped at the expense of someone else's loss.

Let both your speaking and your silence, therefore, be inspired by enlightened love, and wisely guided by your conscious will!

Yet in the end, your silence shall prove more important for your purpose than your speech.

Your way is blest if you shall practice silence wisely.

CHAPTER SEVEN

TRUTH AND VERITIES

IF YOU ARE seeking timeless Truth as the immutable reality that lies beyond all mutable appearance, you needs must learn to differentiate between this deepest, ever-flowing source of Being wherein all Truth abides, and the innumerable verities continuously pouring forth from this all-generating source, in forms forever new and always apt to change.

Only in the realm where Being rests within itself is Truth alike immutable—rooted in its proper ground, a fountain flowing of its own resolve—but infinitely varied are the forms through which that Truth reveals its inner nature in the domain of space and time.

Final Truth as such you could not ever grasp or know; for even in the Spirit's realm it lies eternally beyond all apprehension, wholly inaccessible, save to itself alone.

All life begotten by the "Father," from the boundless wellspring of eternal Truth, is capable of knowing final Truth by virtue only of the same approach: as individuated *self-experience*.

It follows, then, that you as well can only know "one final truth"—one truth you wholly comprehend—the truth that is your own eternal self.

Yet countless verities engulf you on all sides, and each such verity seeks recognition in your mind as a reality expressing final truth.

It often may oppress your own profoundest truth that it is called upon to treat as "truth" what it regards as wholly alien and cannot, without effort, reconcile with its accustomed view.

However, you must not allow this to confound your judgment.

Bear in mind that every truth possesses its own form in space and time, and will conform with nothing more than what that form contains.

You, too, should thus conform with your eternal truth.

That will be achieved, however, when you are master of yourself, so that your thoughts, your words, and deeds at all times are, and will remain, expressions of your own profoundest truth.

Once you know that you yourself are true throughout, you also shall discern those other truths, which earlier had seemed so very "alien." And you shall then discern them in the only way your comprehension ever can perceive them: as aspects integrated with your own eternal truth.

BEAR IN MIND that, veiled within the soul of every human being, there abide all forms of truth, in measureless abundance. And yet, within all that infinity of forms, there only is a single one that can unfold itself in each and every human soul, to grant it certainty and lasting purpose.

You should not, then, pursue one form of truth today, another form tomorrow; for in this way you surely would not ever find the form that is uniquely yours.

That very form you shall attain, however, if you become, as I already said above, completely true in all your thoughts, your words, and deeds—in all expressions of your life.

Whatever in the light of your own truth shall then reveal itself as true will truly be abiding Truth; for falsehood and pretense are powerless where human souls have made their own inherent truth the lodestar of their being.

Still, you see that many people seem convinced of having found the "truth," and yet are clearly in the grip of some deep-rooted error, or of some lie they have not yet unmasked.

Do not begin to doubt yourself in face of their determined blindness, nor let them trap you in the snare of their beguiling "logic."

Again, do not imagine everyone is "evil" who has fallen victim to the false conclusions based upon such sophistry.

Be just, and calmly recognize that the majority of those enthralled by mental phantoms are honestly convinced of having found authentic truth.

To be sure, they all would soon be rid of their delusions if only they themselves would first resolve to make their own lives truthful to the core; instead of letting baseless fictions occupy their minds; phantoms they believe are tangible self-revelations of eternal Truth.

Others you will find so thoroughly subjected to a given verity, that they are quite incapable of contemplating any truth except their own.

If ever you encounter any such, do not be equally intolerant; nor try to force them from the spell of their preferred belief.

Truly, there are many ways that, in the end, can lead a human soul to find its own exclusive truth; indeed, may guide it to become the Truth. But many first must undergo the spell of the most disparate verities before they can awaken, in order to pursue their own inherent truth.

It surely is not easy to be completely true in one's own sight. And if you would attempt it, you soon will grow aware that many times you felt inclined to see yourself as "true" throughout, while in reality there still was much in you that pandered to pretense and empty show.

Again, to be completely truthful does not simply mean to catalogue all one's perceptions and emotions as if one were a mere machine.

Even if you were consistently to keep account of everything you apprehend and feel, and did so with mechanical exactitude and absolute precision, your life as such, considered as a whole, could nonetheless be utterly untrue.

In fact, you must observe a certain "tolerance" between the accurate analysis of your perceptions and emotions, and their interpretation for your understanding. For otherwise it is precisely your obsession with pursuing total truth that will allure you to the sphere of self-deception, where phantom lights abound like specters on a putrid swamp.

Even if you seek to rid yourself of self-deception with relentless zeal you have accomplished very little if all your efforts are directed only at attaining ruthless clarity in the analysis of every feeling that affects your soul.

Your individual judgments may well be wholly accurate in every such examined case; and yet, your life in its entirety, may still present a picture very different from that which one would gain by merely adding up your separate judgments on your feelings and perceptions.

It likewise would be wrong to think one is already truthful if he will only seek to keep his words at all times free of falsehood and of intention to deceive.

To be truthful means above all else that one will always keep one's thoughts securely gathered, lest wishes, fears, or idle dreams should tempt them to forsake the road of sober judgment and aimlessly drift far away, becoming difficult to catch again.

If you are truthful in your thoughts, then all your words and deeds will of themselves bear witness to your inner truth; even if your words should prove in error, and your deeds at times might put you in the wrong.

Trust me, it is better one can prove you guilty of an error or a wrongful deed, committed unintentionally, than of a falsehood toward yourself, even if thereby you had intended to avoid an error or some wrong.

But once you have become completely truthful in yourself, you daily will encounter new and different verities; only now you will no longer find them "incompatible," as you had done before.

You shall discover that, within yourself, you also comprehend the truth of every other human soul. Even though such other truths, in your own life, are but contingent verities; not—like the individuated, central truth of your existence—the guiding light upon your way and the attainment of your goal.

Knowing this will make you tolerant toward other views, and you will not think less of those who do not seek your form of truth in your own way, so long as you can see that they as well pursue their form of truth in their own way.

You then shall recognize that final Truth alone is able to conceive itself as such; although that Truth reveals itself to human comprehension in infinitely varied forms. And even the most distant of these forms still bears the imprint of its timeless source, reflecting light of timeless Truth.

Regard yourself as blessed, knowing that your own eternal truth embodies and reflects degrees of light whose source lies near the heart of absolute and final Truth. Yet, surely, you will not look with disdain on truths of more remote, less luminous reflections, but see instead, in all its infinite degrees of clarity, only revelations of the selfsame One eternal Truth.

CHAPTER EIGHT

CONCLUSION

MOCKERY, which often will diffuse potentially destructive tensions, has justly aimed its caustic barbs at the religious hypocrite, who turned sincere piety into a public exhibition, replete with prayer book and rosary, with eyes devoutly fixed on heaven, and thus appearing as the very pattern of self-righteous affectation.

On the other hand, one must not overlook that, owing to such ridicule, there now are those, and very likely they are many, who can no longer honestly believe that even genuine devotion may have any worth.

Although their sense of piety may well be of the purest kind, they too feel branded by such justified derision, despite its being leveled only at hypocrisy and unctuous cant. And so they almost fear to openly admit how meaningless and shallow they would find a life devoid of true devotion.

One may call it foolish if this concern will cause faint-hearted souls to doubt their truest intuition. And yet, their diffidence is ultimately rooted in the high regard in which they hold true piety; for what such timid souls are typically afraid of is seeing an experience desecrated which they consider holy.

Still, it could be argued that the feelings here at risk are only private and subjective. Perhaps, then, genuine piety is felt to be a real need by only few? A need that only few find truly suited to their nature?

But having promised that my words would guide you in the right direction, on the way toward inner certainty—seeing that you want to know the "meaning" of this present life—I now must also try to show you, in this conclusion of my guidance, that you will never truly comprehend the final meaning of existence unless you are imbued with pure and heartfelt *piety*.

As I already told you earlier, you need to learn a new approach to asking questions. In other words, you should no longer ask about the "meaning" of this present life, but rather how you might yourself inform your life with meaning.

Yet if you phrase your question as I told you, the very best advice I finally can offer you is this: Imbue your soul with pure, profound, and heartfelt piety!

ONLY THUS WILL you endow your life with meaning that shall never cease.

I TRUST, HOWEVER, that you did not merely ask about "the meaning of this life" to satisfy that jaded, commonplace curiosity whose only interest is finding out how mortal human intellect, which is so narrowly restricted even in the wisest of the wise, might reasonably "explain" this physical existence —in order to convince itself.

To entertain such frivolous curiosity is truly not the purpose of my guidance; and little do I care about the selfishly uneasy "children of this world" who ever seem to worry only what they shall have to face in life beyond, instead of acting at all times in such a way that their inheritance can only be a blessing.

Those who feel that this applies to them, may it sting them like a whip, so that they will at last awaken from their torpor, grow mature to reach their highest goal, and gain the right to claim their spiritual heritage.

IF I DISCUSS the fact that you are able to give "meaning" to your present life, I chiefly seek to make you understand that your existence here on earth, which in itself results from the inexorable consequences of countless prior causes, in turn becomes the cause of many more such consequences. And I would have you recognize that here it lies in your own power to determine the direction of those consequences, insofar as you are able to transform the tenor of your earthly life.

It is not a question simply of evoking lofty inner feelings, let alone of fostering the infantile and vain belief that you are chosen to perform some "mission" in this life, and that your every action here is of extreme significance to God.

On earth you may be the most powerful and most exalted among mortals—the scion of an ancient line, the heir of ruling dynasties, possessing boundless wealth—yet in the eyes of those who weigh eternal worth your person, as a mortal creature, remains a wretched little worm that one unwary step may crush to death, even if the heart enlivening that step would gladly spare your life.

The transformation of your temporal existence, through which you likewise shall transform your life to come, requires more of you than merely elevating your sense of personal importance from the world of physical existence to that of everlasting life.

Whether in this mortal life you are the loftiest of potentates, or the most wretched of all beggars, in either case you need to understand that all these things are finally irrelevant, have no concrete existence in the eyes of those who are the Spirit's kings and priests—the Spirit whose reality is rooted in its radiant substance—although they will respect your standing and accomplishments in this external life, to the extent you make their recognition possible.

WHAT IS DEMANDED of you by the Spirit's law is conscious, carefully considered action.

The demands you have to meet are not by any means "excessive."

You merely need to demonstrate that you are earnest in your quest. And you can prove your resolution only by employing the power you are given over things on earth in such a way that you acquire "treasures" in your life beyond which neither "moth nor rust" are able to "corrupt."

There will be no "exemption," nor any "commutation" of what the Spirit's law demands; however much Eternal Love would like to grant you both—as you undoubtedly believe is proper.

Again, be very careful not to think that you perhaps could cheat a little, or deceive eternal law, by seemingly performing what is being asked of you, while disregarding things that go against the grain of what your creature selfishness desires.

There is no "judge above" who will "condemn" you. For it is *you* who will pass judgment on *yourself*: by virtue of the way you put to use what is entrusted to your power here on earth.

If you are poor, you may be certain that whatever you create out of your poverty shall not be held of lower worth than the impressive contribution of the wealthy. On the other hand, if you are rich and live in splendor, the works that you performed on earth shall weigh no more upon the Spirit's scale than they appear commensurate with your potential.

Being rich, you are expected to contribute your proper share of things that you were given, in order to increase the Spirit's "working capital" within this world of visible reality.

It is for you to know how much the Spirit of eternity, from which your own existence stems, expects you to contribute in material coin: on earth, where values are material. And you shall surely not make progress on your inner path if you avoid performing your full share, also in respect to matters of material worth.

It is clearly not a question of "distributing" your worldly goods. Rather, the extent of your possessions will determine what you can contribute to establish spiritual values in this present world. In the same way that your earthly wealth provides the measure for your other contributions.

The Spirit's law expects no more of you than that your quest for inner light comprise your outer life as well. So, that the full potential you are granted in this outer world be dedicated to the service of eternal life.

At no time are you called upon to offer more than you are able to perform, without neglecting obligations you must meet in your external life.

Yet there will surely come a day when you would bitterly regret your having disregarded what the Spirit's law demands.

GIVEN THAT you never can escape from being part of all-embracing life in the eternal, it is doubtless only prudent to adjust your life—already in your days on earth—according to the law that governs life in the eternal.

After all, your very presence in this mortal world is consequent upon your own eternal life, which is not in the least affected by any doubts you might indulge concerning its reality.

There is no other way for you to lend true meaning to your present life than by your seeking to experience its reality, with open heart and conscious mind, as an integral part of your eternal life.

You only can achieve that goal, however, if you can rid yourself of the invidious illusion that would beguile you to believe that you shall one day consciously experience everlasting life, even if you failed to structure also your experience of this earthly life according to the laws that govern all eternity.

If you would lend abiding purpose to your life on earth, be sure that everything you undertake is always done in such a way that it will likewise further values of a higher kind.

For, in the end, your present life will have true meaning only if it continues being fruitful, and if its harvest shall be yours to reap for all eternity.

REMINDER

"Yet here I must point out again that if one would derive the fullest benefit from studying the books I wrote to show the way into the Spirit, one has to read them in the original; even if this should require learning German.

"Translations can at best provide assistance in helping readers gradually perceive, even through the spirit of a different language, what I convey with the resources of my mother tongue."

From "Answers to Everyone" (1933), *Gleanings*. Bern: Kobersche Verlagsbuchhandlung, 1990.

By the same author:

The Book on the Living God

Contents: Word of Guidance. "The Tabernacle of God is with Men." The "Mahatmas" of Theosophy. Meta-Physical Experiences. The Inner Journey. The En-Sof. On Seeking God. On Leading an Active Life. On "Holy Men" and "Sinners." The Hidden Side of Nature. The Secret Temple. Karma. War and Peace. The Unity among Religions. The Will to Find Eternal Light. Mankind's Higher Faculties of Knowing. On Death. On the Spirit's Radiant Substance. The Path toward Perfection. On Everlasting Life. The Spirit's Light Dwells in the East. Faith, Talismans, and Images of God. The Inner Force in Words. A Call from Himavat. Giving Thanks. Epilogue.

The Kober Press, 1991. 333 pages, paperback. ISBN 0-915034-03-4

This work is the central volume of the author's *Enclosed Garden*, a cycle of thirty-two books that let the reader gain a clear conception of the structure, laws, and nature of eternal life, and its reflections here on earth. The present work sheds light on the profound distinction between the various ideas and images of "God" that human faith has molded through the ages—as objects for external worship—and the eternal *spiritual reality*, which human souls are able to experience, even in this present life. How readers may attain this highest of all earthly goals; what they must do, and what avoid; and how their mortal life can be transformed into an integrated part of their eternal being, are topics fully treated in these pages.

What sets this author's works on spiritual life apart from other writings on the subject is their objective clarity, which rests upon direct perception of eternal life and its effects on human life on earth. Such perception is only possible, as he points out, if the observer's *spiritual* senses are as thoroughly developed to perceive realities of timeless life, as earthly senses need to be in order to experience *physical* existence. Given that authentic insights gathered in this way have always been extremely rare, they rank among the most important writings of their time, conveying knowledge of enduring worth that otherwise would not become accessible.

The Book on Life Beyond

Contents: Introduction. The Art of Dying. The Temple of Eternity and the World of Spirit. The Only Absolute Reality. What Should One Do?

The Kober Press, 1978. 115 pages, paperback. ISBN 0-915034-02-6.

This book explains why life "beyond" is not so much a different and wholly other *life*, but rather the continuation of the self-same life we live on earth. The difference between the two dimensions lies chiefly in the organs of perception through which the same reality of life is individually experienced. On earth we know that life through our mortal senses, in life beyond it is perceived through spiritual faculties, which typically awaken after death. At that transition, the human consciousness, which usually is unprepared for the event, is at a loss and finds itself confused by the beliefs and concepts of its former mortal life. As a result, the new arrival faces certain dangers; for, owing to these mental prejudices, the person is unable to distinguish between perceptions of objective truth and the alluring phantom "heavens" generated by misguided faith on earth.

To help perceptive readers form correct and realistic expectations, that they may one day reach the other shore with confidence and without fear, this book provides trustworthy guidance into spiritual life, its all-pervading structure, laws, and inner nature. Given the unbreakable connection between our actions here on earth and their effects on life beyond, the book advises how this present life may best prepare the reader for the life that is to come.

The Book on Human Nature

Contents: Introduction. The Mystery Enshrouding *Male* and *Female*. The Path of the Female. The Path of the Male. Marriage. Children. The Human Being of the Age to Come. Epilogue. A Final Word.

The Kober Press, 2000, 168 pages, paperback, ISBN 0-915034-07-7

Together with *The Book on the Living God* and *The Book on Life Beyond*, *The Book on Human Nature* forms a trilogy containing guidelines toward a new and more objective understanding of both physical and spiritual realities, and of the human being's origin and place within these two dimensions of creation.

The Book on Human Nature at the outset shows the need to draw a clear distinction between the timeless spiritual component present in each mortal human, and the material creature body in which the spiritual essence is embodied during mortal life. The former, indestructible and timeless, owing to its being born of spiritual substance, represents the truly *human* element in what is known as mortal man. The latter, physical, contingent, and subject to decay and death, is no more than the temporary instrument the spiritual being uses to express itself in physical existence. Given that the spiritual and animal components within human nature manifest inherently discordant aspects of reality, they typically contend for domination of the total individual. Experience shows that in this conflict the animal component with its ruthless drives and instincts clearly proves the stronger.

To help the reader gain a realistic understanding of the human being's spiritual and physical beginnings, by way of concepts more in keeping with humanity's advances in every discipline of natural science, the book explains, to the extent that metaphysical events can be conveyed through language, the timeless origin and source of every human's spiritual descent. It likewise shows that the material organism, now considered mankind's primal ancestor, existed long before it was to serve the spiritual individuation as its earthly tool. In this context the author points out that the traditional creation story, such as it has survived, is not simply an archaic myth, invented at a time that lacked the benefits of modern knowledge, but instead preserves, in lucid images and symbols, a truthful view of actual events. Events, however, that did not happen merely once, at the beginning of creation, but are a process that continues even now, and will recur until this planet can no longer nurture human life.

Even so, the principal intention of the present work, as well as of the author's other expositions of reality, is not so much to offer readers a new, reliable cosmology, but rather to encourage them to rediscover and awaken the spiritual nature in themselves, and thus to live their present and their future life as fully conscious, truly *human* beings.

The Book on Happiness

Contents: Prelude. Creating Happiness as Moral Duty. "I" and "You". Love. Wealth and Poverty. Money. Optimism. Conclusion.

The Kober Press, 1994. 127 pages, paperback. ISBN 0-915034-04-2.

Sages and philosophers in every age and culture have speculated on the nature, roots, and attributes of happiness, and many theories have sought to analyze this enigmatic subject. In modern times, psychology has joined the search for concrete answers with its own investigations, which frequently arrive at findings that support established views. Still, the real essence of true happiness remains an unsolved riddle.

In contrast to traditional approaches, associating happiness with physical events, the present book points to the spiritual source from which all human happiness derives, both in life on earth and in the life to come. Without awareness of this nonmaterial fundament, one's understanding of true happiness is bound to be deficient.

The author shows that real happiness is neither owing to blind chance, nor a capricious gift of luck, but rather the creation of determined human will. It is an inner state that must be fostered day by day; for real happiness, as it is here defined, is "the contentment that creative human will enjoys in its creation." How that state may be created and sustained, in every aspect of this life, the reader can discover in this book.

The Book on Solace

Contents: On Grief and Finding Solace. Lessons One Can Learn from Grief. On Follies to Avoid. On the Comforting Virtue of Work. On Solace in Bereavement.

The Kober Press, 1996. ISBN 0-915034-05-0.

In this book the author shows how sorrow, pain, and grief, although inevitable burdens of this present life, can and ought to be confronted and confined within the narrow borders of necessity. Considered from the spiritual perspective, all suffering experienced on this earth is the inexorable consequence of mankind's having willfully destroyed the state of perfect harmony that once had governed nature. Although the sum of grief thus brought upon this planet is immense, human beings needlessly expand and heighten its ferocity by foolishly regarding grief as something noble and refined, if not, indeed, a token of God's "grace."

Understanding pain objectively, as a defect confined to physical existence, which, even in exceptional cases, is but an interlude in every mortal's timeless life, allows the reader to perceive its burdens in a clearer light, and thus more patiently to bear it with resolve.

While suffering, through human fault, remains the tragic fate of physical creation, the highest source of solace, which helps the human soul endure its pain and sorrow, continually sends its comfort from the Spirit's world to all who seek it in themselves. How readers may discover and draw solace from that inner source the present book will show them.

The Wisdom of St. John

Contents: Introduction. The Master's Image. The Luminary's Mortal Life. The Aftermath. The Missive. The Authentic Doctrine. The Paraclete. Conclusion.

The Kober Press, 1975. 92 pages, clothbound. ISBN 0-915034-01-8.

This exposition of the Fourth Gospel is not a scholarly analysis discussing the perplexing riddles of this ancient text. It is, instead, a nondogmatic reconstruction of the actual events recorded in that work, whose author wanted to present the truth about the Master's life and teachings; for the image propagated by the missionaries of the new religion often was in conflict with the facts. The present book restores the context of essential portions of the unknown author's secret missive, which the first redactors had corrupted, so that its contents would support the other gospels.

Written by a follower of John, the "beloved disciple," its purpose was to disavow the "miracles" the other records had ascribed to the admired teacher. His record also is unique in that it has preserved the substance of some letters by the Master's hand, addressed to that favorite pupil. Those writings are reflected in the great discourses which set this gospel text apart and lend it its distinctive tone.

Given the historic impact of the man presented in this work, an accurate conception of his life and message will not only benefit believers of the faith established in his name, but also may explain to others what his death in fact accomplished for mankind.

About My Books, Concerning My Name, and Other Texts

The Kober Press, 1977. 73 pages, paperback. ISBN 0-915034-00-X.

This book presents selections from the author's works that let the reader gain a clear conception, both of the spiritual background and perspective of his writings, and of their extraordinary range and depth. For readers seeking knowledgeable guidance through the labyrinth of speculations, dogmas, and beliefs concerning *final things*, his expositions will provide a source of comfort and enduring light.

And since, from the "perspective of eternity," human beings bear responsibility to practice spiritual discernment, lest they be deceived by falsehoods, readers here will find reliable criteria to clarify their own beliefs regarding mysteries that neither mental powers nor religious faith have ever fully answered.

By showing that objective knowledge of spiritual existence is not only possible, but that attaining such experience is finally the foremost task of human life, these books become essential guides for readers seeking inner certainty, which mere belief cannot create. In this respect it is the practical advice these books provide which is their most remarkable characteristic.

Spirit and Form

The Kober Press, 2000.

The underlying lesson of this book is that all life in the domain of spiritual reality, from the highest to the lowest spheres, reveals itself as lucid order, form, and structure. Spirit, the all-sustaining radiant *substance* of creation, is in itself the final source and pattern of all perfect form throughout its infinite dimensions. Nothing, therefore, can exist within, or find admittance to, the Spirit's inner worlds that is devoid of the perfection, harmony, and structure necessarily prevailing in these spheres.

Given that this present life is meant to serve the human being as an effective preparation for regaining the experience of spiritual reality, this life must needs be lived in ways that are consistent with the principles that govern spiritual reality; in other words, ought to be lived according to the structure, laws, and inner forms of that reality. To show the reader how this present life receives enduring form, which then is able to survive this mortal state, the book sheds light on crucial aspects of this physical existence and advises how these may be formed to serve one's spiritual pursuits.

THE
KOBER
PRESS